21/21

Chad Carpenter

BookLeaf
Publishing

India | USA | UK

Presentation by *BookLeaf Publishing*

Web: www.bookleafpub.com

E-mail: info@bookleafpub.com

ISBN: 9789357214964

First edition 2023

ACKNOWLEDGEMENT

These works would not be possible without my experiences on this beautiful planet over the past four decades. Hard or easy, these trials and tribulations, both light and dark, have helped shape me into the person I am today.

My friends, family, past loves, and community taught me several lessons. I am forever grateful for these experiences and look forward to finding balance on this planet with people and the nature around me.

If I had one wish for the world, is to remind everyone we're more alike than different and are all in different places on our journeys. It's essential for each of us to remember and celebrate life and to lift those around us.

PREFACE

21/21 is a collection of poems that explores the author's relationship between love, life, and finding his way in the world. This poetry grouping is taken from different parts of my life between 2001 and 2022.

Headspace

A thousand words,
cluttered thoughts,
moving throughout,
A substrate of space and time.

What is current, long past,
All that I can't seem to leave behind.

Containment.
Takes practice.

A memory.
A feeling.
A lost connection.
Reconnected.
Purpose.
Drive.

All in due time.
Trust, said process,

No patience, keep searching,
But what will I find?

What is the moral lesson that I must learn,
this time?

A thousand words, no structure,
A blank page sits on the table,
Wordless and eager to be defined.

Candlelight

A dark room is given light,
The warmth of its heat,
Removes the chill from the night.
The source is calm, steady, bright,
Softens the shadows,
As it crackles and flickers,
Dancing in its unique light.
The hue is amber, blue,
and deep shades of green,
Bringing something unique to this night,
A chance to sit, breathe,
meditate peacefully,
Under the single flame— candlelight.
An opportunity for one's self to be still,
calm, steady, and bright,
It brings peace, thought, clarity,
Watching the candle burn,
Oh, so bright.
Do not waste its magical light,
As for now,
This candle provides,
Much more than just,
Light.

A title of another time

Songs play,
no words to say,
You appear,
Strange.

We say goodbye,
We don't cry,
Forever.

Stationary in a parking lot,
shuffling songs,
smiling,
Sensual moments,
Saltwater and skylines,
Nightfall.

We choose to be distant.
With little to no words.

Tahoma

Mammoth Mountain,
Tahoma, Tacoma,
or Tacobet,

Beautiful and brilliant.

Glaciers glisten,
Sun-cast shadows,
Dance amongst the trees,

Western Hemlock,
Douglas-fir,
And the mighty cedar trees,

She tells an important story,
of our rich Pacific Northwest History,

She is the keeper,
Of many majestic secrets,
Revealing them in space and time,

She creates a vital habitat,
For marmots, warblers, and bobcats,

Simply divine.

While it's been roughly 130 years
since your last outburst,
You're not quiet by any means.

Constant and quietly shifting, shaping,
growing over time.

Thank you, mother mountain,
For sharing your rich ecosystem,
With us--the outdoor enthusiasts,
Allowing us to enjoy all you offer,
from babbling brooks to scenic drives,

May you continue to provide.

The Senses

At first sight,
I knew you were special,
An instant connection,
without conversation,

Sharing just eye contact,
Your beautiful eyes shared,
A lifetime of stories,
Of wonder, excitement,
And fortunes untold,

A silent trust built by sight alone.

Fragrance top-notch,
Setting pheromones ablaze,
You enticed, created arousal,
Embody comfort,
Encouraged sensual play.

For you,
Words run easily,
You have a great sense of style,
Kind,
Caring,
Empathetic,

Not to mention,
A gorgeous smile.

From past car rides to music,
It was easy to stay,
At the present moment,
Listening away,

Your lips are soft,
Exploratory,
Most likely refined,

The first time you touched me,
I knew you were different,
Slow, thoughtful, and full of intention.

Thank you for the senses.

My partner in 26 words

Adventurous
Broad-Minded
Communicative
Dynamic
Enlightened
Flexible
Generous
Humorous
Insightful
Judicious
Kind
Likable
Mirthful
Neat
Optimistic
Passionate
Quick-witted
Remarkable
Sensible
Thoughtful
Unique
Vivacious
Warm-hearted
X-tra
Youthful
Zestful

Passage of time

Sometimes life feels like it's moving too
quickly,
Tilted on its axis,
Like the vintage merry-go-round,
Round and round,
We tend to ask ourselves,
 "Will this ever stop?"

And sometimes life feels like it's moving too
slowly,
Tic toc, tic toc,
You can hear nothing,
But second-hand,
Movement of the clock.

Other times, life feels like it's moving just right,
You can look around, hear the sounds,
Of laughter, birds, and everyday chatter,

Learn to enjoy each passing moment,
From the quiet to the loud,
For it will end too soon,
And perhaps, when we're not ready.

The Looking Glass

The mirror,
A solid flat surface,
Spell-bounding to the eye,

The mirror,
Can you help remind us,
Of where we've been,
And what we've become,

The mirror,
Tells a fraction of the whole story,
As light bounces, Images prevail,

The mirror,
Maybe incapable of truth,
But it will never lie,

The mirror,
Cannot express,
Cannot feel,
It is only an illusion,
Created in one's mind.

The mirror,
Often shares,
multiple sides.

Adventure

An adventure awaits,
It's time to pack up,
And play,

To the forests,
Mountains,
Ocean or beach,

Best to stay present,
Focus,
And just be,

Still in your thoughts,
Standstill,
Just remember to breathe,

Let your guard down,
Allow yourself,
A few moments,
To let go and be free,

Create laughter,
Make memories,
Be inspired by the,
World around,

Take in,
An extra moment,
For yourself to process,

Remember this moment,
When life gets you down,

Embrace the feels both,
The ups and the downs,

Always make time for adventure,
There are many to be found.

Seaside

Seagulls, sand, and surf,
Eateries and ebb tides
Anchor signs, Algae, and Anemones.
Sails, starfish, and saltwater taffy
Ice cream, intertidal zones.
Dune buggy, docks, and a place to dive.
Eagles.

All things to see along the sea.

Reflection

Deep thoughts,
Reflexive moments,
Bring clarity,

Moments of highs,
Followed by lows,

Shame.

Beautiful relationships,
Big growth.

Lost.

Seven years, solo,
Built walls,
Trust shaken.

Alone.

Feeling proud,
Living now,

Creative.

Reconnecting,
Learning to love,

Rebounding.

Looking forward,
To live life,
Full.

Inspired.

Photographs

A beautifully bound photo album,
Rests on a shelf,
Tells a story of great moments past,
An image,
Time stands still.

Some in color, sepia, and in black and white.

In the garage,
A lone dusty box, shelved high,
Holds memories of days gone by,
Dust stirs,
Polaroids, Kine, Kodak,
Painted gloss images,
Reveal a past cast,
Of characters,

Others present.

Stirring thoughts,
Evoking Emotions,
Images captured,
Youth immortalized.

Trips, travels, and sights.

Reconnecting us to
A time that's gone by.

Winter Mountain

In the distance,
A rustic cabin,
Mountaintop,
A small light burns bright.

A plume of gray smoke billows,
From the weathered stove pipe.

Alpine greens, small twiggy trees,
A rack of multi-colored skies and poles,
Vertical near the side door.

CAT tracks in the snow,
Show a path,
This must be the hub,
A place to gather, and
Warm by the fire.

Laughter is heard in the air,
A blissful time of year,
For the winter fair,
Outdoor activities,

Slopes full,
Boards, skies,

And tubes at play.

Bundle up, and take flight,
For it's a winter's delight.

Squall

Gentle gusts sing,
A blast of Arctic breeze,
Gale force increases,
Wind howls,

A barrage of agitation,
A roar of the ocean floor,
At the onset of the intense waves,
Build in the distance,
And land on the soft surf.

A crash on the breakwater,
Creates a magnificent eruption,
Fine mist and spray surround,
The rock-filled jetty.

The roll of thunder,
It creates an intense sound,

This day is blustery, gray,
And life seems a bit quiet,
While observing this small,
Beach-themed town.

Tomorrow will be different,

Waves will calm,
Winds peaceful,
Sunshine,

A perfect day to fly a kite.

Loyalty

A generous being,
Second to none,
Loyal to a fault,
Waivers for no one.

Observant,
Caring and kind,

My heart is always,
Pinned to my sleeve,

A patchwork of colorful flannel,
Tells my fable,

I am seldom quiet,
And favor on-the-go,

Should you fall,
I'll answer the call,
Day, night,
Matters not.

Goofy, awkward at times,
Adventures abundant,
Uncontrollable laughter,

Lifting others,
All in due time,

I'm here to inspire.

Ready

When will I be ready?
To receive love in abundance,
Stay true to your thoughts,
And intentions.

My mind is ready,
My heart beats steady,

Build comfort from within.

By writing and working,
Learning and growing,

For it will come when ready,
Keep focused and open,

Live in the moment,
Take chances,
Stay vulnerable.

Foster growth,
And ask for help,
It's ok to fail,
But keep hope.

Day by day,
Steady and true,
Inspire, create,
Be bold.

Scatter love,
Along the way.

Fear

Don't overproof fear,
It can propel one forward,
Or hold one back.

Fear helps to protect,
A warning signal,
To be careful,
And cautious.

Be open,
Expand the view,
And broaden our minds.

Fortify the bond.
Focus on Breathing,
Recognize the excuses.

Buying into fear
Slows us down
And builds fences,

Barriers.

Do new things
Let go, if not serving,

Be comfortable with change,
And reap the rewards.

For, in the end, life is a path,
With lots of undiscovered trails.

Do not fall into fear.

Bailey-pup

A beautiful, brindle,
Baby-angel,
Entered my life,
So long ago.

Not sure I was ready,
Or what I was doing,

We've been through,
So much,
From beginning
Up to now,

You seem to anticipate,
My every move,
With a wag.

You are an independent,
Patient and curious creature,

You tell tall tales, from days long ago,

Always kept watch,
With your best ball, blanket,
and bed in tack,

To be quite honest,
I'm not sure,
Who saved who.

I'll be forever grateful,
As you've taught me so much,
From patience to
poop-scooping.

I'll never be able to repay you,
Not that you ever asked me to,

I'm glad we've connected,
through and through,

We've created some fantastic memories,
That I'll cherish til the end.

You have given me an abundance of love,
When I needed it most,
And in return,
You've only asked for a scratch and bone.

Thank you,
Miss Bailey,
You are simply the best,

I wish you relaxation,

In your remaining days,

Just sit and enjoy,
The back porch,

And by all means,
Bark away!

Pops

Thank you for sharing,
A big gift with me,
One so precious,
It will never leave.

Whether spent,
In the barn, garden, or woodshed,
There was always some life lesson,
That felt like a session,
Bestowed onto me.

From telling big stories,
In the Midwest,
From Omaha or Great Falls,
From large cornfields and popcorn,
White Buffalos to cars,

I enjoyed them all.

From late-night firesides,
Or known as 'nightcaps' to some,
Time spent together,
It was second to none.

These stories are there to teach us,

An important lesson or two,
What things do we carry,
And what lessons carry us through,

Life is too short,
We must enjoy what we do,
Celebrate the highs,
And learn from the lows,

As I left for work each day,
you'd be the first to exclaim,
"CHAD, MAKE IT A GOOD DAY!"

Thank you for the life lessons,
Reminders, and of course,
All the love.

I'm proud to be your fifth,
and your only adopted kid!

The honors are all mine,
Thank you for giving me,
The best gift called time,
I've learned so much,
That I'll carry on.

I love you, Pops.

What are your words?

At thirty-four,
The first word was jealousy,
To remove and release,
Felt so liberating.

At thirty-five,
The second was patience,
To sit, breathe, and let go,
Rinse and repeat,
Time and time again.

At thirty-six,
Calmness came on the scene,
A chance to remain cool, calm, and collected,
Or better known as level-headed.

At thirty-seven,
With a sense of purpose,
A reason, an intention,
It's just what we do!

At thirty-eight,
Truth.
A constant opportunity,
To be open to one oneself,

Honest, raw, and authentic.

At thirty-nine,
Balance was on my mind,
What received too much time,
Versus, not enough,
Work versus home,
Live versus pursuits.

Creating boundaries.

At forty,
Came a chance to create,
New colors, new tools,
And a new decade to ring in.

At forty-one,
Brought great connection,
A chance to reconnect,
From the past to the present,
Learning to live without regrets.

At forty-two,
Finding challenge,
In staying present,
For a Gemini soul,
Likes shiny,
And sometimes,
It takes practice to stay focused.

At forty-three,
Seeking adventure,
It is the only way to go!
Traveling,
And learning,
Connecting and growing.

At forty-four,
It is to inspire,
To fill the gaps and
Feel the reactions,
Of doing good.

These are my value words,
That I concisely practice.

They keep me on track,
And moving forward,
Ten years, ten words,
That has shaped,

My foundation.

Cinquain

36

Brown Eyes
Live your journey,
Impact from the ground up,
Intellectual, honest, and bright,
We vibe.

www.ingramcontent.com/pod-product-compliance
Lightning Source LLC
LaVergne TN
LVHW051238200726

843510LV00011B/1604